for 1000+ tutorials ... use our
free site .... drawinghowtodraw.com

BY RACHEL GOLDSTEIN

HOW TO DRAW COOL THINGS, OPTICAL ILLUSIONS, 3D LETTERS, CARTOONS AND STUFF

A Cool Drawing Guide for Older Kids, Teens, Teachers, and Students

BOX RISING OFF OF PAPER

Here is a cool 3-dimensional effect that is quite simple to draw. It really will look like a cute square is rising off of the paper.

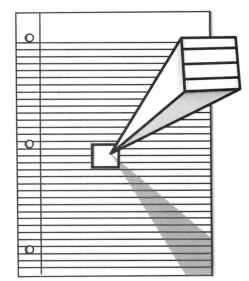

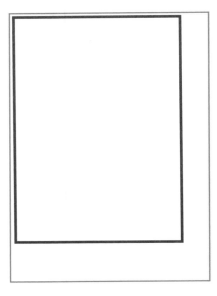

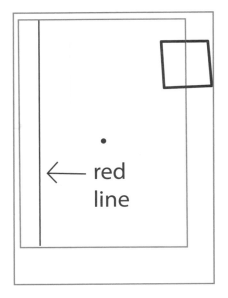

← red line

1. Draw a rectangle on the upper left side of a piece of paper.

2. Draw a light red line along the left side of the rectangle. Draw slightly slanted rectangle on right side. Draw a dot on the page.

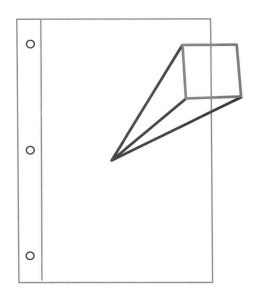

Draw lines from the rectangle down to the point you drew. Draw 3 circles on left side of page.

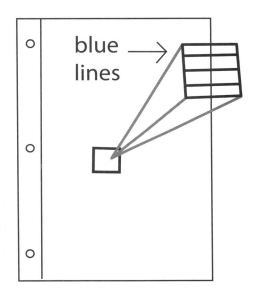

blue lines →

4. Draw a smaller rectangle around the point. Draw 3 blue lines on the bigger rectangle.

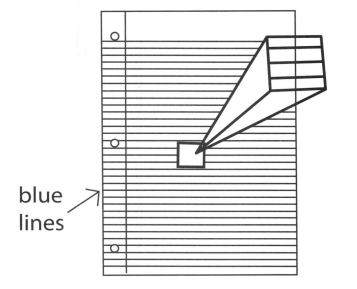

blue lines ↗

5. Draw blue lines around the shapes that you drew.

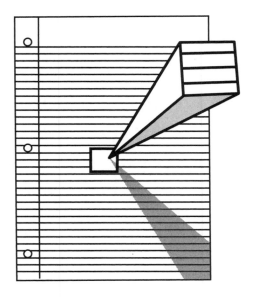

 Draw a gray cast shadow by drawing 2 outward slanted lines that form a triangle. Fill it in gray. You should be able to see the lines thru the shadow. Use a lighter gray to shade the right side of the paper tower.

Shade the left side of the holes + rectangle

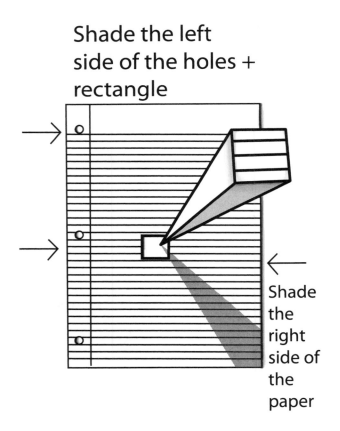

Shade the right side of the paper

Add some very light shading to the top of the paper tower. Add darker shading to the right side of the piece of paper, as well as the left side of the paper holes and the cut out rectangle.

GUY FALLING OFF YOUR PAPER

This is a cool drawing trick that will amaze your friends. It will actually look like a cartoon boy is hanging off of your paper. Find out how below.

1. First of all, you need to draw a cartoon boy on the right side of a piece of paper turned on its side. We will show you how to draw him below.

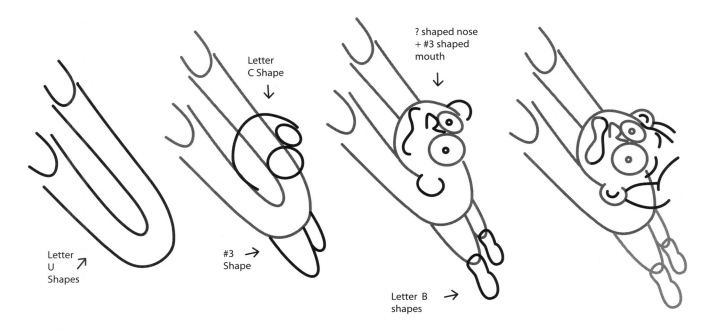

Letter
U
Shapes

Letter
C Shape

#3
Shape

? shaped nose
+ #3 shaped
mouth

Letter B
shapes

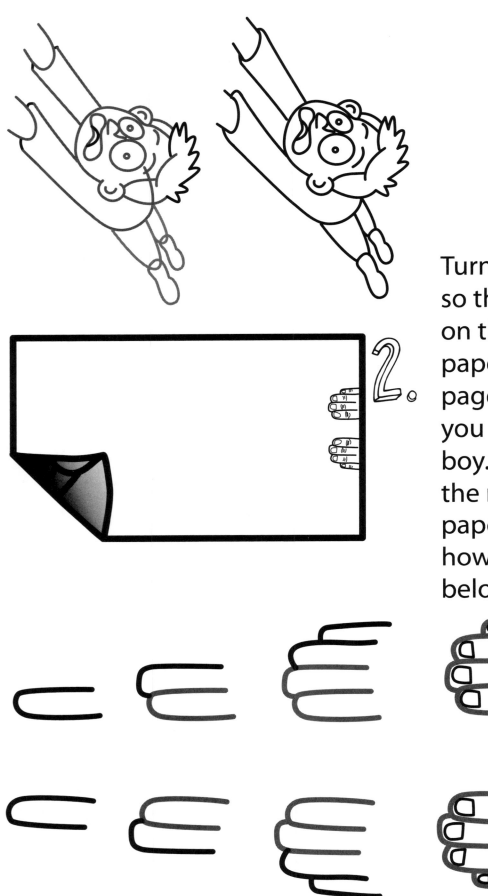

Turn over the page so that the boy is on the bottom of the paper. If you lift the page up on the left, you should see the boy. Draw hands on the right side of the paper. I show you how to draw hands below.

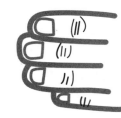

3. Now roll / curve the paper over and match up the hands with the arms. It will look like a 3d person is hanging off of your paper! Cool... isn't it?!!!

CELTIC KNOT

Start off with dots and end up with a really cool Celtic knot. It couldn't be easier to draw something so cool!

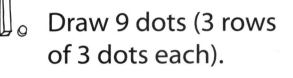

1. Draw 9 dots (3 rows of 3 dots each).

2. Now draw 4 dots at the very top and bottom. Space the dots around the previous dots.

3. Now draw 2 more rows of 4 dots.

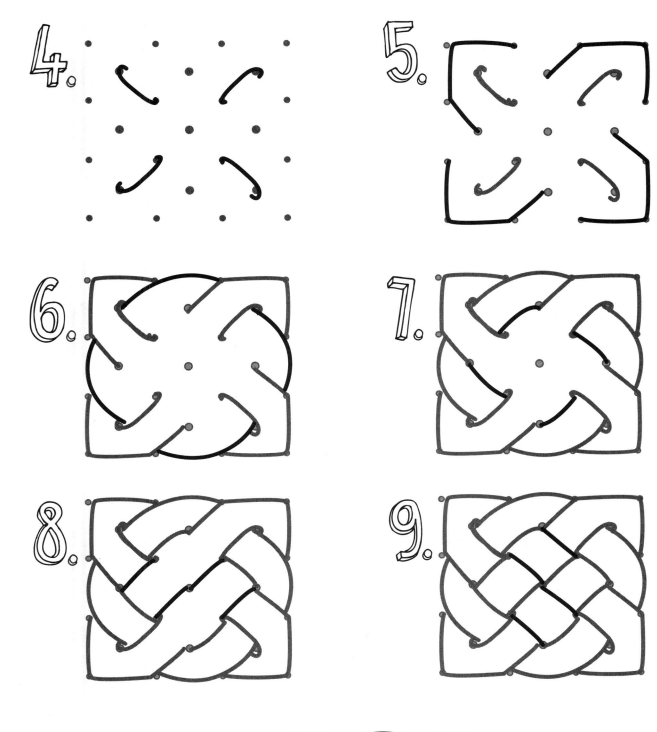

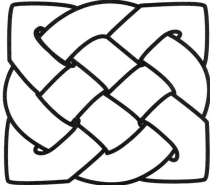

IMPOSSIBLE SQUARE

The impossible square on the right probably makes your brain hurt. We will show you how to draw this optical illusion below.

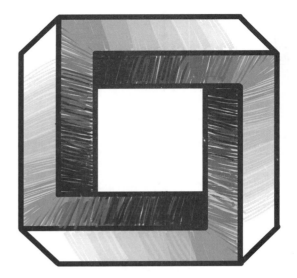

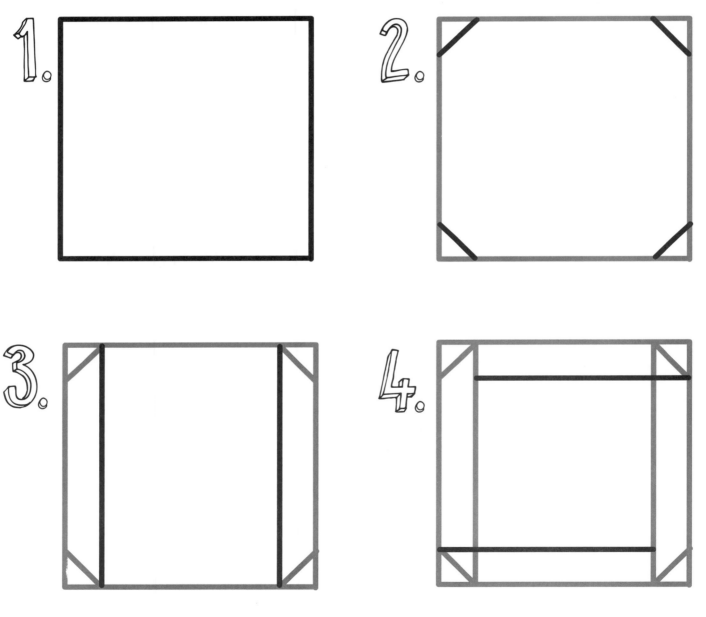

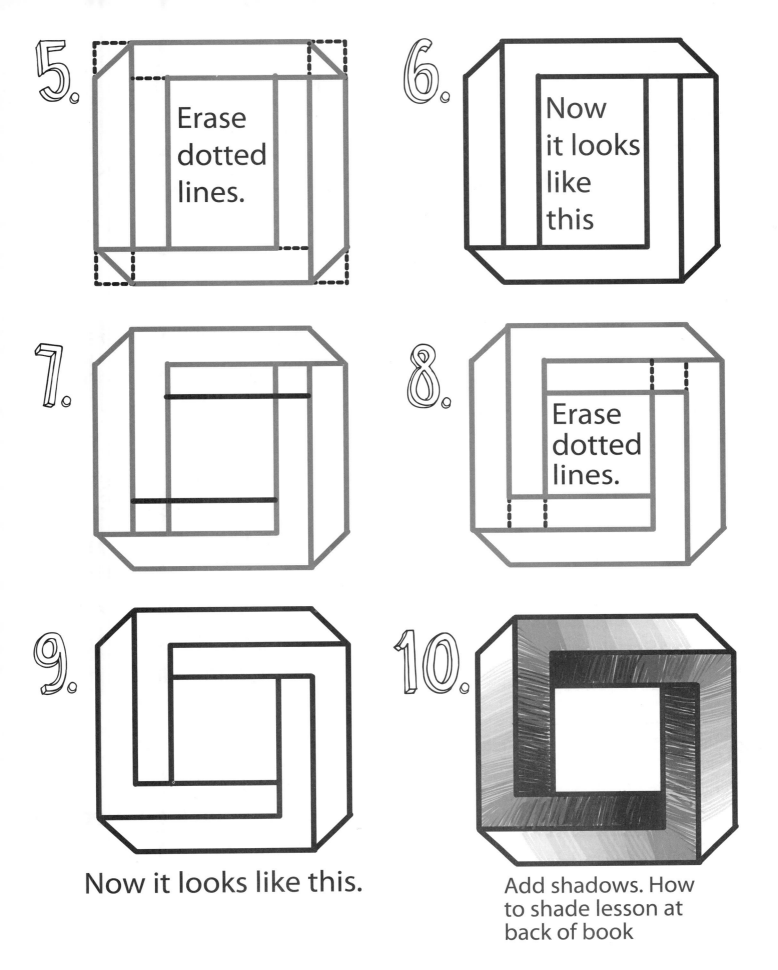

5. Erase dotted lines.

6. Now it looks like this

7.

8. Erase dotted lines.

9. Now it looks like this.

10. Add shadows. How to shade lesson at back of book

FOLDED PAPER LADDER

This looks so amazing when it is completed. The ladder that you draw will look like it is floating in between the folded piece of paper. Super cool!

1.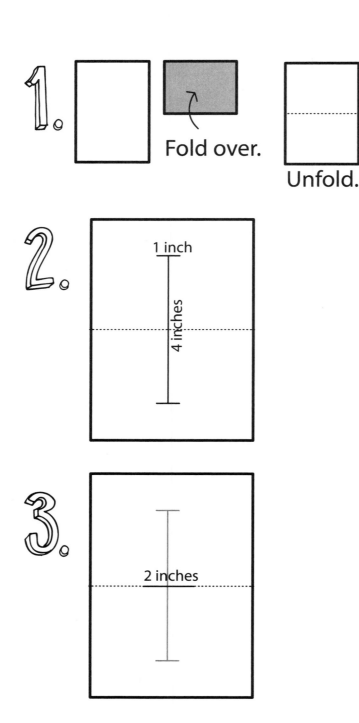

Fold over.

Unfold.

Fold a piece of paper. Unfold it.

2.

1 inch

4 inches

Draw a line 4 inches tall (2 inches above the fold and 2 inches below it). Draw a 1 inch line centered at the top and one at the bottom of the 4 inch line.

3.

2 inches

Draw a 2 inch line on the fold (centered on the 4 inch line).

4.

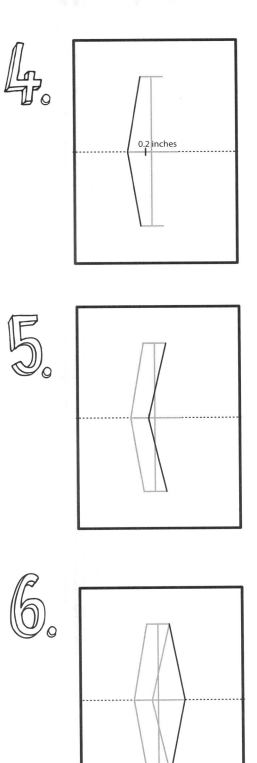

0.2 inches

Draw a line connecting the left-most parts of the lines that you drew. Draw a notch or dot 0.2 inches (or 0.5 cm) left of the center line.

5.

Draw a line from the right-most part of the top line, down to the point that you drew in step #4. Then Continue the line down to the right-most part of the bottom line.

6.

Draw a line connecting the right-most parts of the lines that you drew.

7.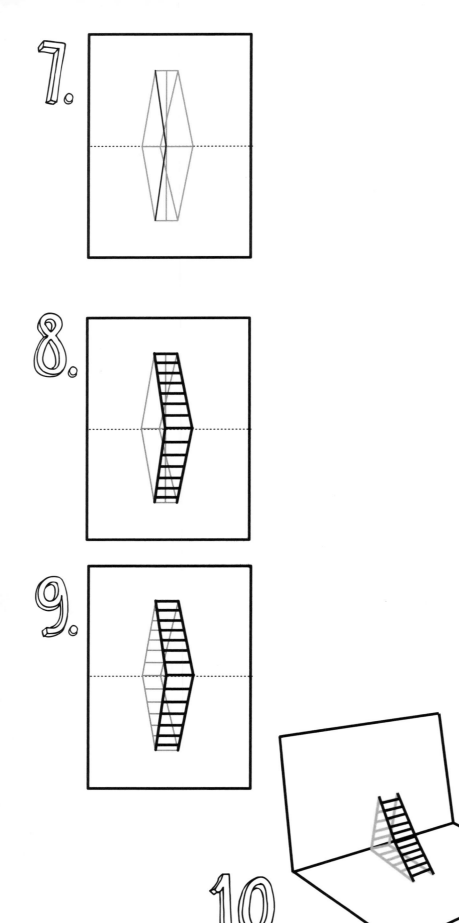

Draw a line from left-most part of the top line to the exact center. Continue the line down to the left-most part of the bottom line.

8.

Darken some of the lines. Draw lines across for the ladder's steps.

9.

With gray, draw the shadows of the steps.

10.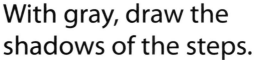

Fold the paper like this to see the 3d effect come to life! So cool!

3D RIPPLES / FOLDS

These ripples and folds look really hard to draw, but just follow along with this lesson and you will be drawing them too.

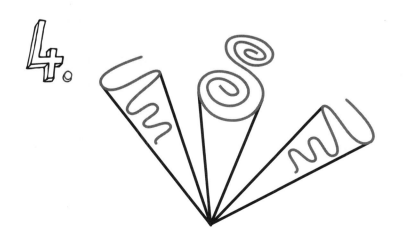

1. 2. Draw a letter "S". Then continue the curved lines to form spirals within it.

3. Draw wavy, curvy lines on both sides of the letter "S" shape. Then draw a dot below everything.

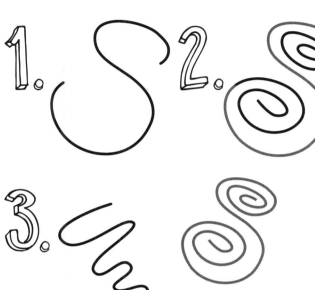

4. Draw lines from the outer edges of the shapes, down to the dot that you drew in step #3.

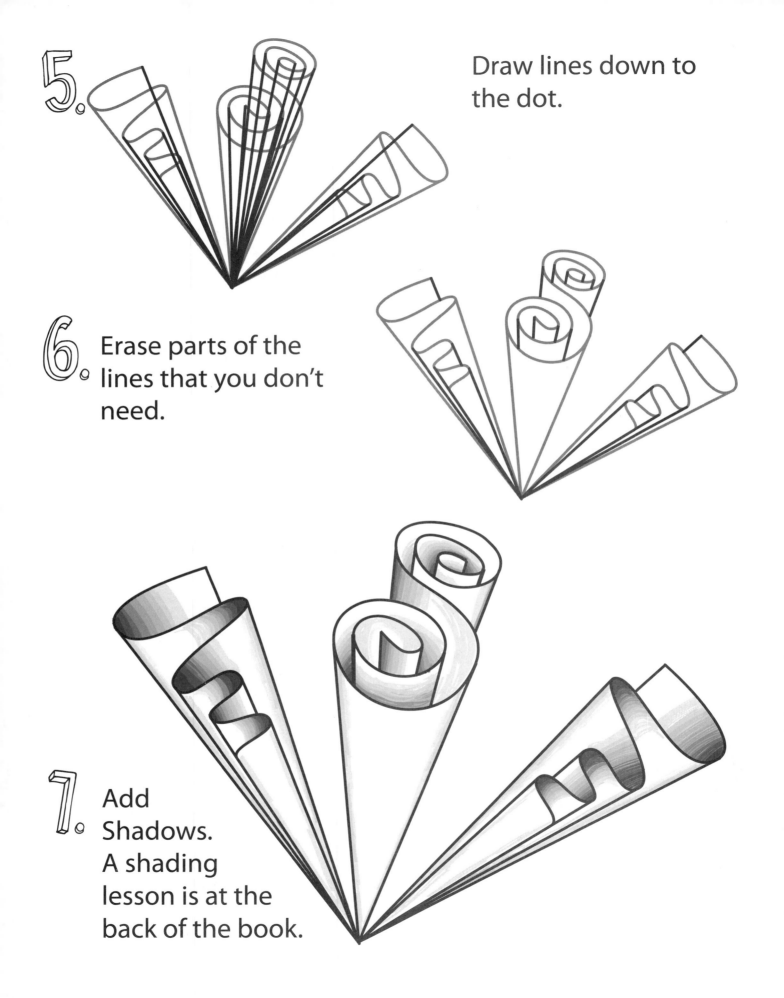

5. Draw lines down to the dot.

6. Erase parts of the lines that you don't need.

7. Add Shadows. A shading lesson is at the back of the book.

3D HEART

Find out how to draw
this 3-dimensional heart.

1.

Draw a heart.

2.

Draw lines all around
the heart.

3.

Draw curved lines
in between the lines,
as seen in the picture
to the left.

4.

 5.

 6.

Add light shadows to the right and left side of the heart. And a small shadow at the top center as well. There is a shading lesson at the back of the book.

Add darker shadows on outer right edges of the heart to make it look like it is above the paper.

3D STACKED BOXES

You have most likely seen this 3D design before. Now you can learn how to draw it yourself. It is super easy to draw and looks really cool when it is complete.

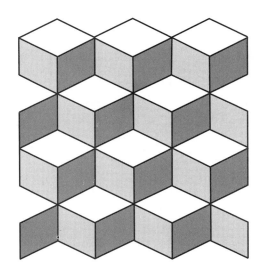

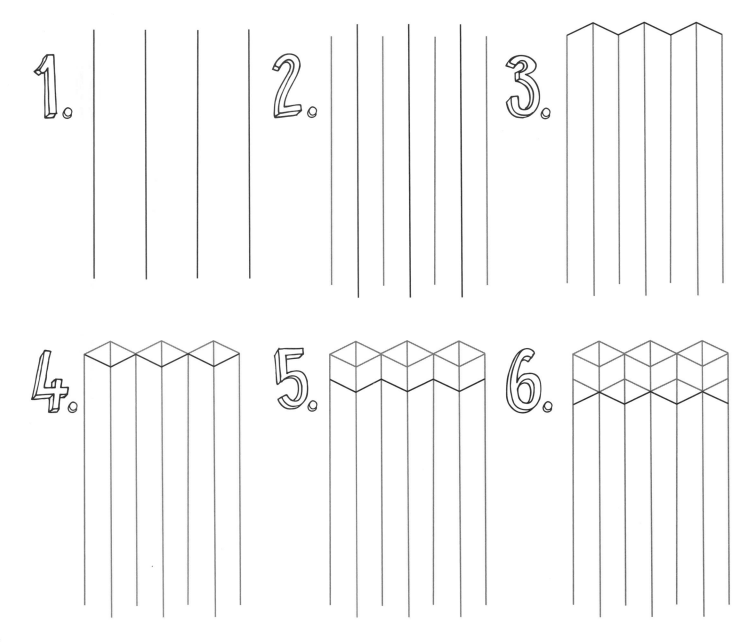

7.

8.

9.

10.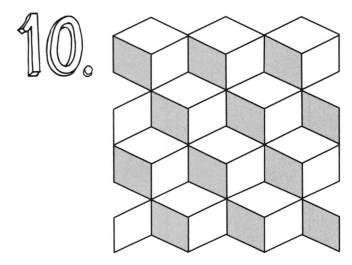

Color in the left side of the boxes with light gray.

11.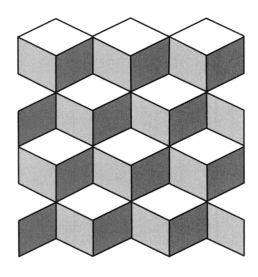

Color in the right side of the boxes with dark gray.

To draw these 3-dimensional letters, you use one point perspective techniques. This is super easy to draw and comes out really cool.

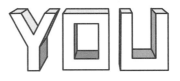

1.

Draw a dot in the center of the page. At the top of the page draw block letters (Go to the back of the book to see how to draw block letters).

2.

Draw lines from the bottoms of the top letters down to the center dot.

3.

Draw lines from the tops of the bottom letters to the center dot.

4.

Figure out how wide you want your letters to be. Draw a horizontal line at the location you want it to be.

5.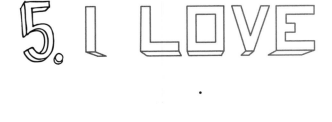

Erase the parts of the lines that you don't need any more.

6.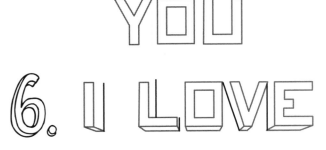

Draw some of the lines that will be the backs of the letters.

7.

Draw some more lines down to the center dot. These lines will be the sides of the letters.

8.

Erase parts of the lines that you no longer need.

9. I LOVE

YOU

Draw more lines that are part of the backs of these letters.

10. I LOVE

YOU

The letters should now look like this.

11. I LOVE

Color in some parts light gray and other parts dark gray.

FLOATING CUBE

Learn how to draw this anamorphic cube. This is a difficult tutorial, but the results are amazing. The cube will really look like it is floating!

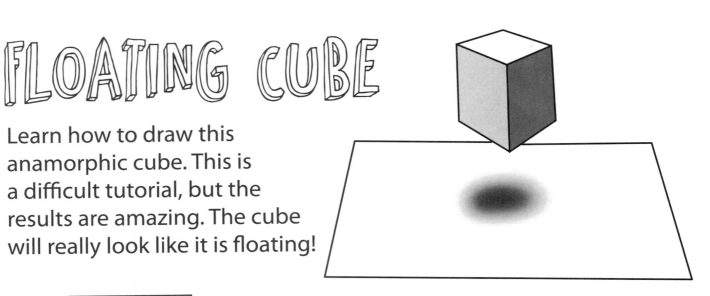

1.

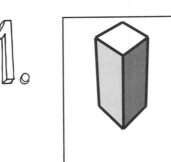

Draw this very specific 3D rectangle at the top of a piece of paper. I will show you how below.

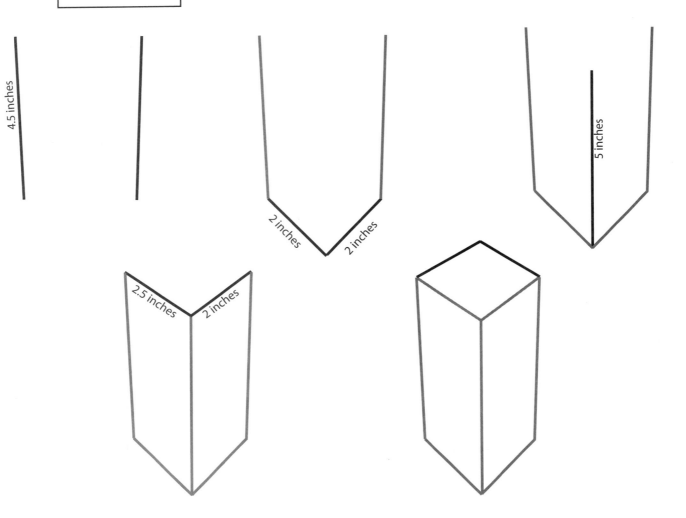

2.

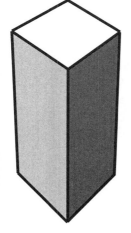

Add light gray to the left side and dark gray to the right side.

3.

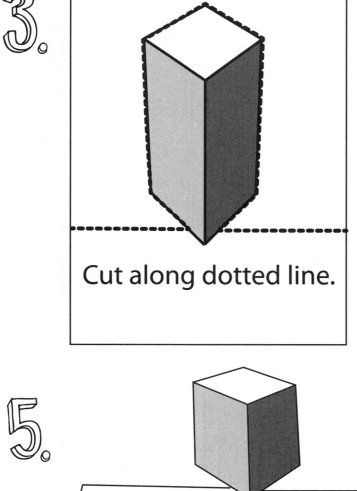

Cut along dotted line.

4.

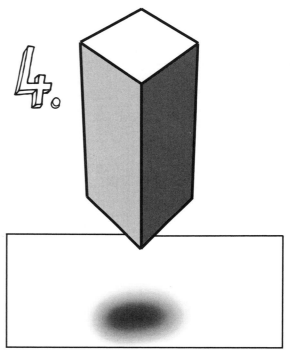

Draw an oval shadow underneath the cube.

5.

Move away from your paper. You will notice that as you back up, the tall tower turns into a floating cube. Cool!

HAIR BRAID

A lot of people struggle with drawing braids. This is the easiest way I know of drawing braids. Lets see if you can draw braids now.

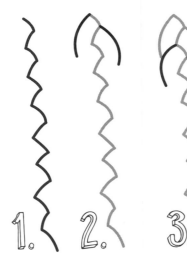
1.

2.

3.

4.

5.

6.

7.

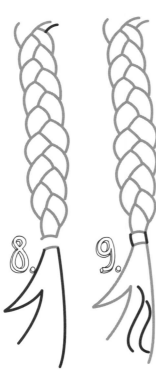
8.

9.

10.

11.

12.

IMPOSSIBLE STAR

This star is an optical illusion. Learn how to draw this complicated star with the following instructions.

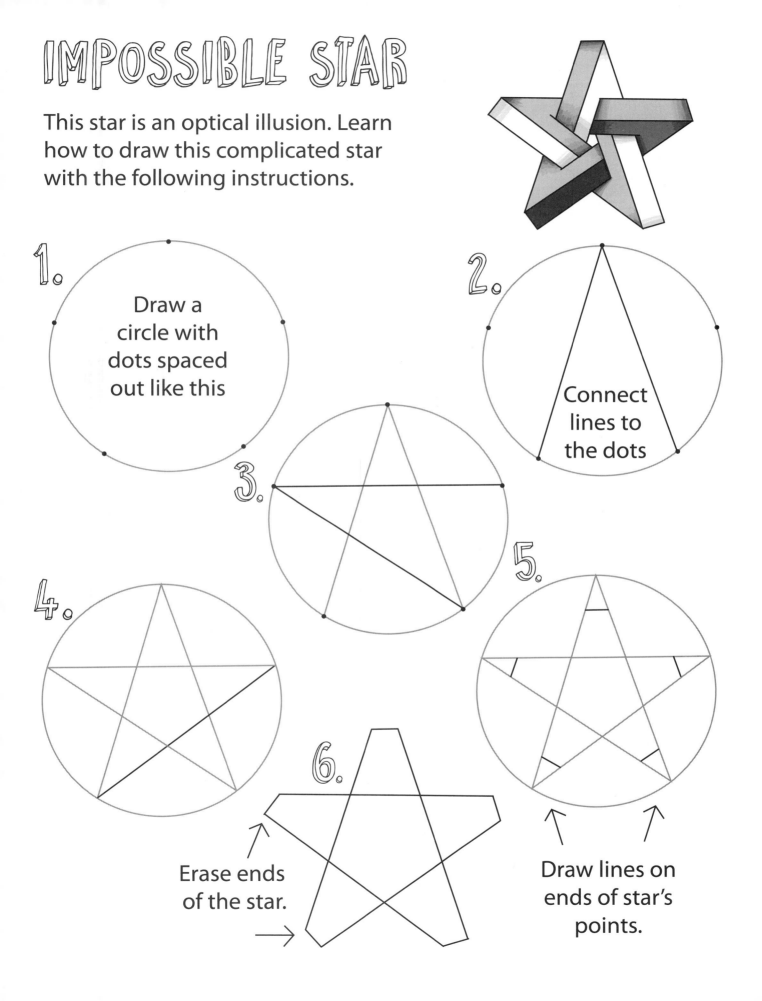

1. Draw a circle with dots spaced out like this

2. Connect lines to the dots

3.

4.

5. Draw lines on ends of star's points.

6. Erase ends of the star.

7.

8.

9.

10.

11.

Erase the
dotted lines.

12.

13.

14.

Erase the
dotted lines.

15.

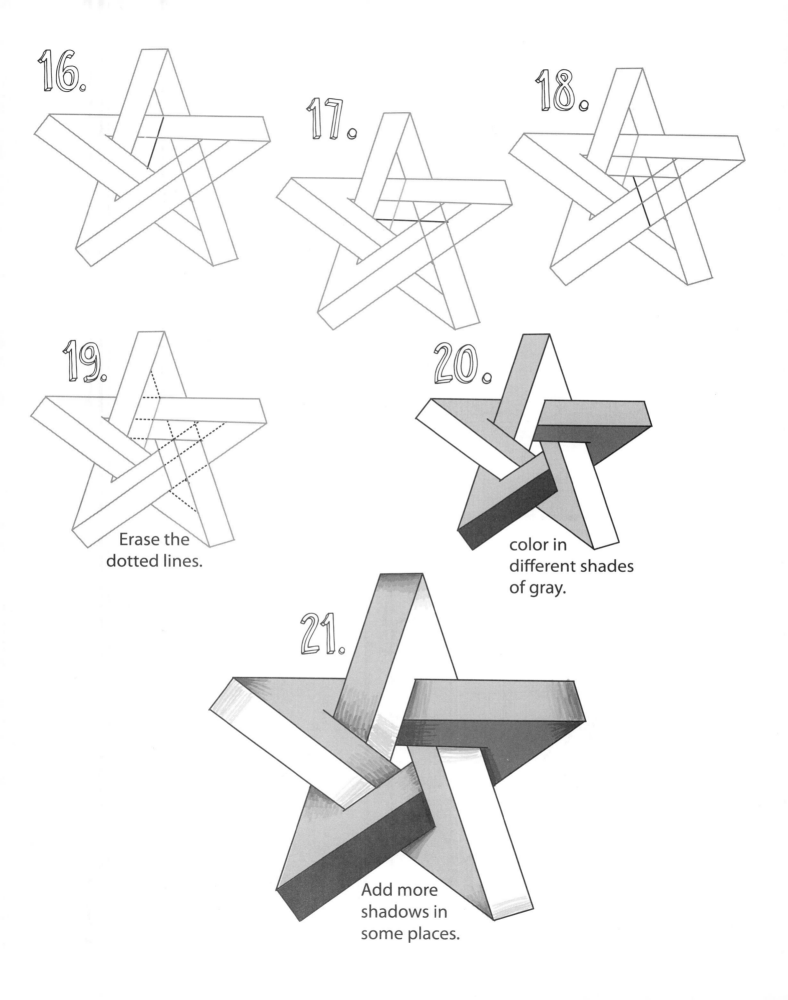

16.

17.

18.

19.
Erase the
dotted lines.

20.
color in
different shades
of gray.

21.
Add more
shadows in
some places.

FISH ATTACK

A fun 3D trick to make it look like a big fish is about to eat a swimmer up. Cool stuff!

1. Take a piece of paper and draw a fish on one end and a swimmer on the other end. I show you how to draw these characters below.

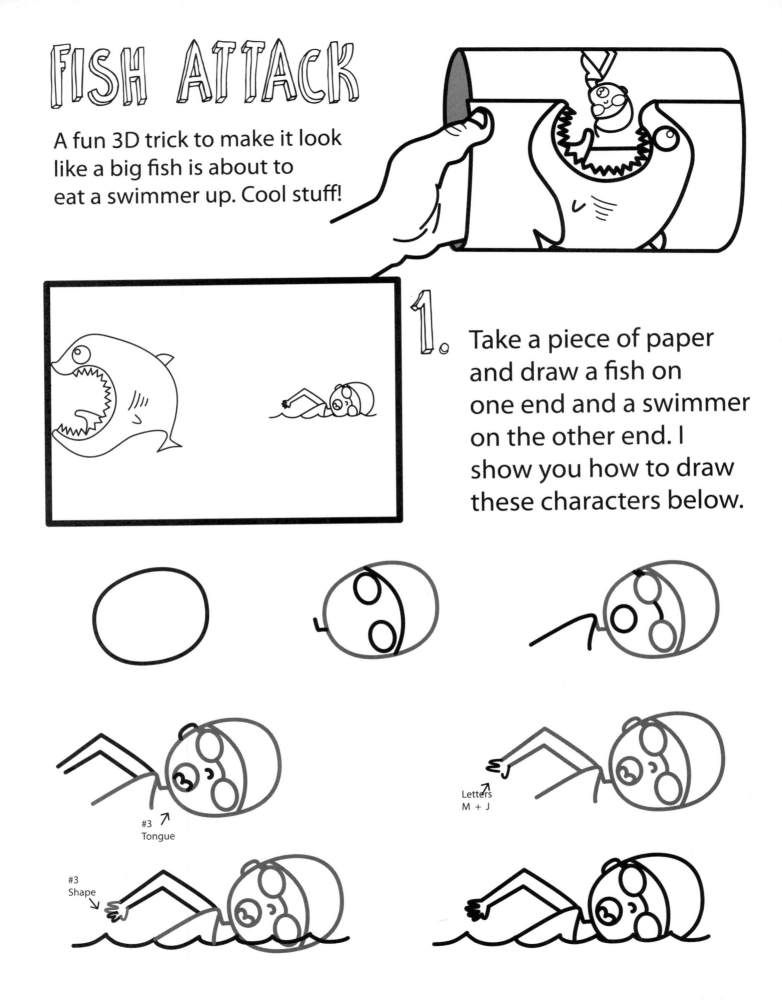

#3
Tongue

Letters
M + J

#3
Shape

Letter
C
Mouth

Letter
M ↗
Teeth

Letter
S
Shape
↓

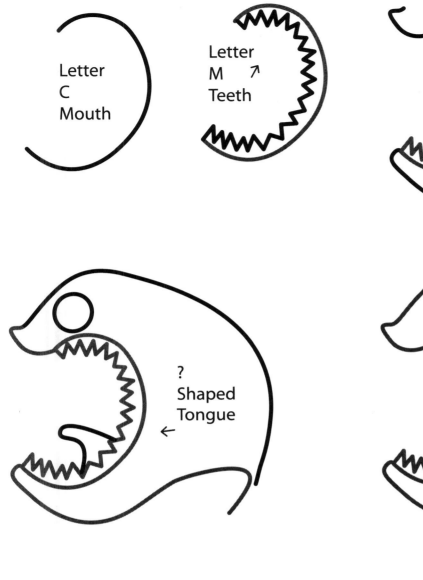

? Shaped
Tongue ←

#7 →
Tail

2.

Cut out the inside of his mouth

3.

Now roll the piece of paper and make it look like the swimmer is about to be eaten by the fish. Think up your own 3d roll drawings, such as a boat going into a tunnel, a bird flying into a cat's mouth, etc.

PEEL UP LETTER

This letter "H" looks like it was cut out of paper and is being pulled out. It looks really cool and is a great thing to doodle when you are bored.

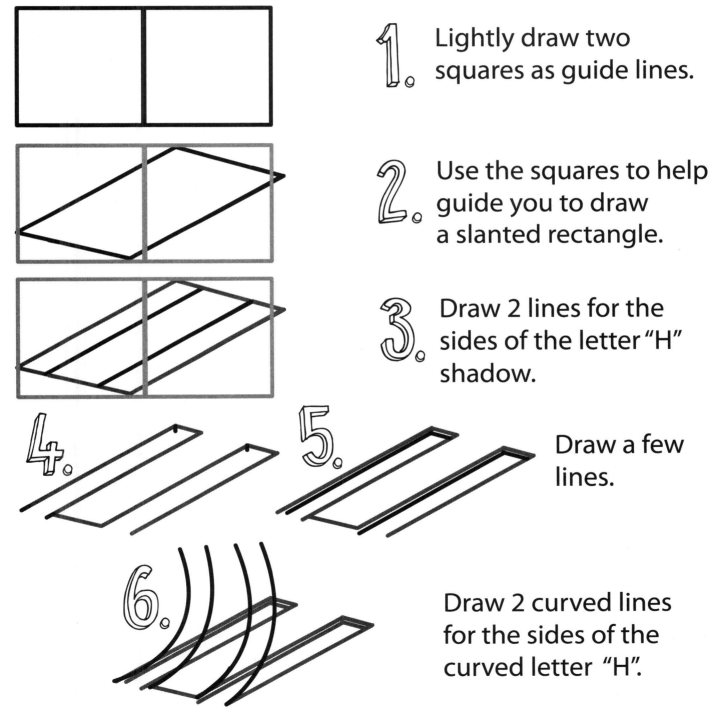

1. Lightly draw two squares as guide lines.

2. Use the squares to help guide you to draw a slanted rectangle.

3. Draw 2 lines for the sides of the letter "H" shadow.

4.

5. Draw a few lines.

6. Draw 2 curved lines for the sides of the curved letter "H".

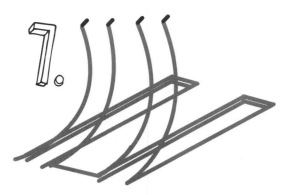 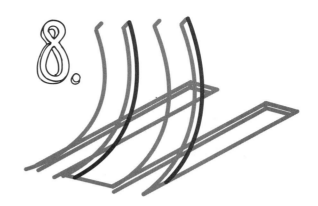

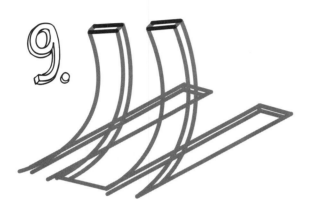 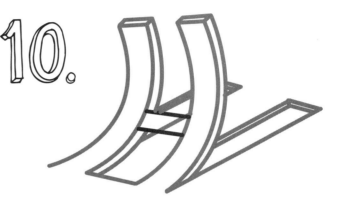

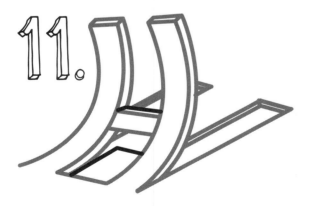 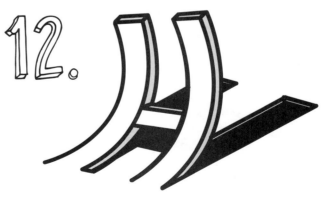

Fill in with gray and black to make it look realistic.

BROKEN WALL REVEALING BRICK

Here is a cool trick to draw a broken wall that reveals some brick showing through. This looks like it would be really hard to draw, but it isn't too bad. Super cool wall!

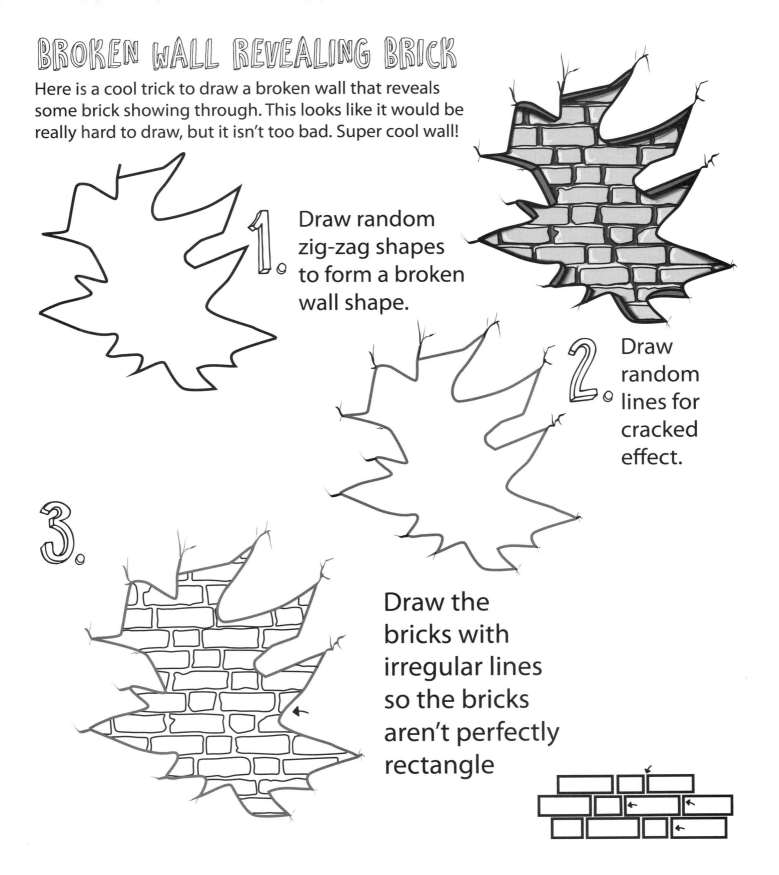

1. Draw random zig-zag shapes to form a broken wall shape.

2. Draw random lines for cracked effect.

3. Draw the bricks with irregular lines so the bricks aren't perfectly rectangle

Make sure that vertical white spaces don't match up with ones from above or below!

Shade in the
bricks a light gray.

Shade the sides
of the wall
dark gray.

8.

Shade in the sides of the bricks. It should get darker the further back the brick goes.

9.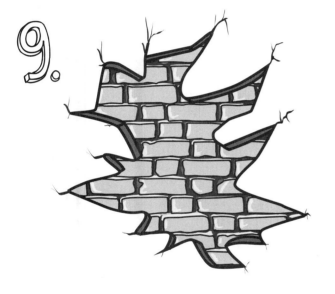

Take a white pencil and color in the tops of the brick white. Also put a little bit of white at the bottom left side of the bricks.

10.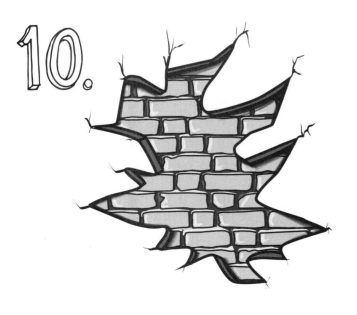

In order to make it look like the bricks are behind the wall, you should put a shadow beneath it. At the top, the shadow is below the wall. At the bottom, the shadow is above the wall.

 CURVED LETTERS

Here is a cool trick to make it look like your letters are curving off of the page. Cool!

 HELLO

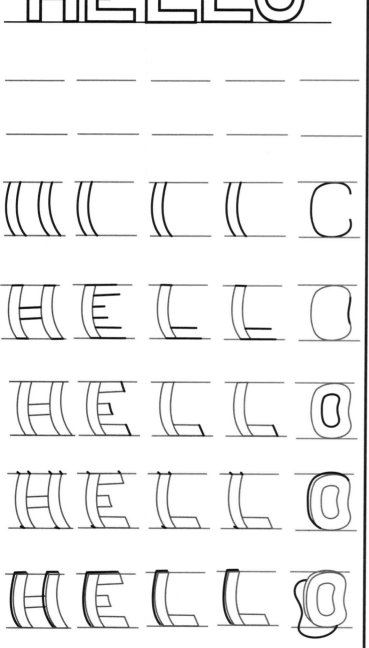

1. Don't draw this. I am just showing you what the letters look like normally.

2. Take a ruler and space out room for 5 letters.

3. Draw curved lines for the "H", "E", "L"s. For the "O" draw a letter "C" shape.

4. Draw lines on the "H", "E", and the "L"s. For the "O" draw a wavy line to finish the outer shape.

5. No changed to the "H". Draw lines on the "E" and the"L"s. For the "O" draw the inner line.

6. Draw lines on the "H", "E", and the "L"s. For the "O" draw a curved line on the left side.

7. Draw curved lines on the left side of the "H", "E", and the "L"s. For the "O" draw a backwards #3-like shape on the left side.

8. Now draw curved lines in the opposite direction. Draw two curved lines inside the "O".

9. Draw some lines.

10. Finish up the drawing.

11. Fill in the space with dark gray.

12. Add some shading to the top of each letter to make it look like they are curved forward.

RIBBON

Ribbons are hard to draw, but I have broken it down in a way that will make it easy for you to learn.

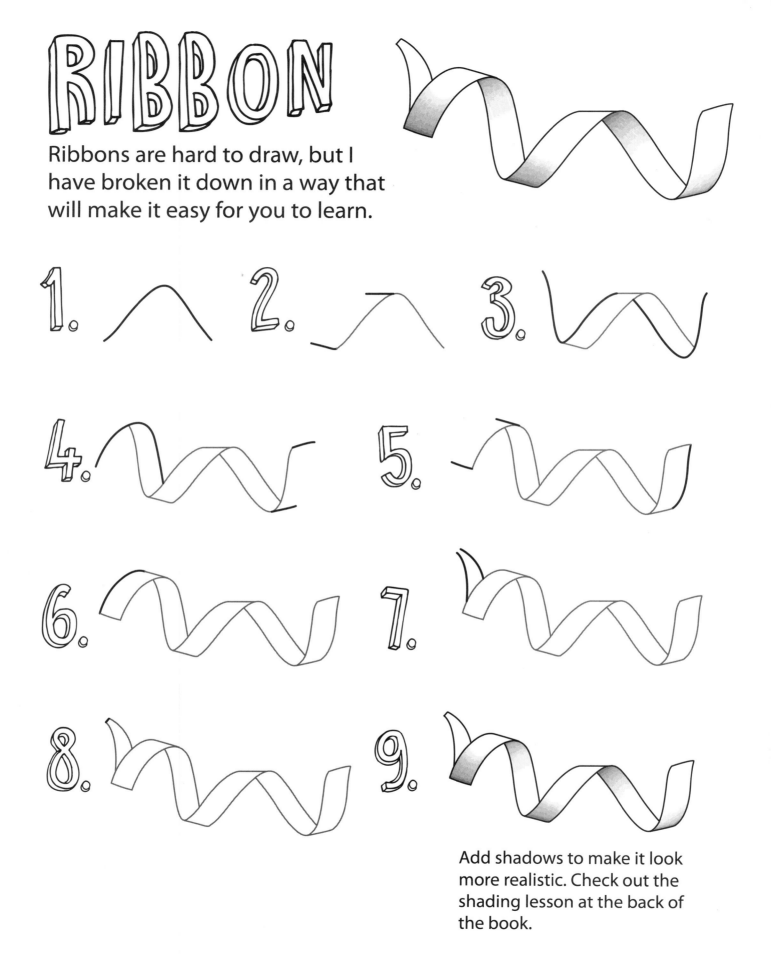

1.

2.

3.

4.

5.

6.

7.

8.

9.

Add shadows to make it look more realistic. Check out the shading lesson at the back of the book.

WATER DROPS

Learn how to draw water droplets and tears on gray paper. This is a cool trick that will make you look like a drawing genius!

1.

Go get some gray paper. The gray paper will make this much easier for you.

2.

Lightly draw the outer shapes of the droplets.

3.

Use a white colored pencil to draw highlights.

4.

Draw a shadow on the right side of each droplet.

5.

Lightly shade in parts of the droplets, as I have.

6.

Smudge the shading a bit...if you have a Q-tip, this works best.

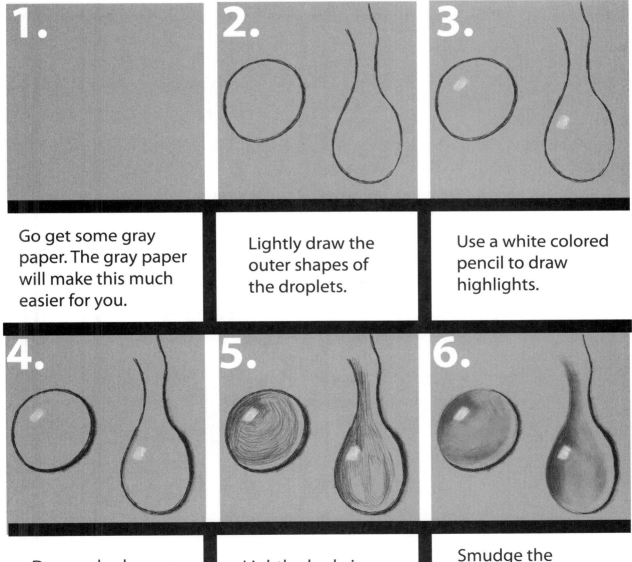

7.

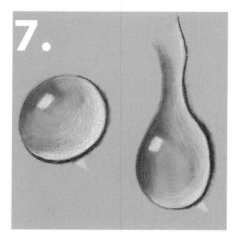

Add some white highlights, including triangle highlights.

8.

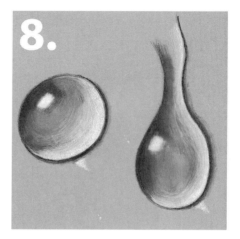

Add some dark shadows and then smudge it a bit.

9.

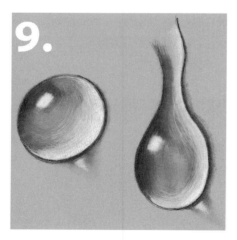

Add some shadows around the triangle.

10.

Add some white to blend all the shading together.

SPIRAL COIL

This is something that everyone should learn how to do. Drawing a spiral vine or coil is a fun thing to doodle when your teacher is being soooooooo boring. Cool!

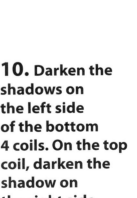

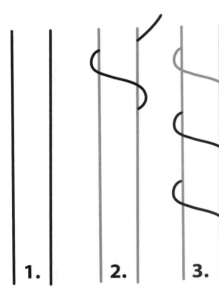

1.

2.

3.

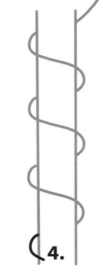

4.

5.

6.

7.

8. Draw a gray shadow at the left side of everything, except for the top coil (which is on the right side).

9. Draw a shadow on the top left side of each of the bottom 4 coils. Also draw a shadow below each of the letter "S" shapes.

10. Darken the shadows on the left side of the bottom 4 coils. On the top coil, darken the shadow on the right side.

IMPOSSIBLE TRIANGLE

This impossible triangle is made up of tiny cubes. It is a really cool effect that will really make your friends think that you are an artistic master!

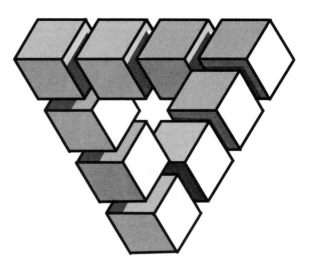

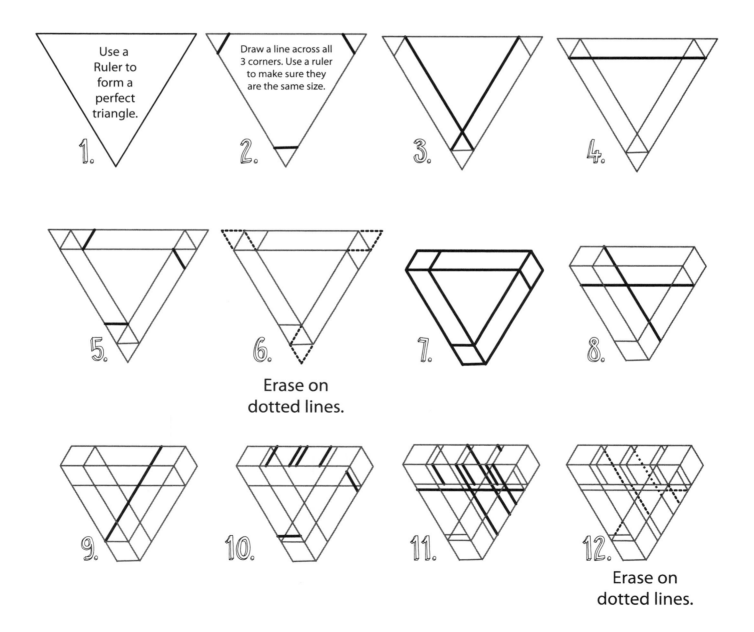

1. Use a Ruler to form a perfect triangle.

2. Draw a line across all 3 corners. Use a ruler to make sure they are the same size.

3.

4.

5.

6. Erase on dotted lines.

7.

8.

9.

10.

11.

12. Erase on dotted lines.

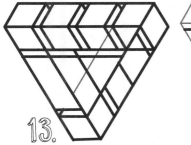

13.

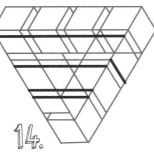

14.

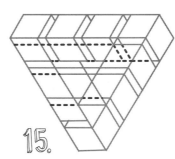

15.

Erase on
dotted lines.

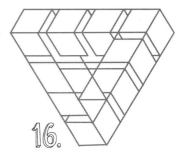

16.

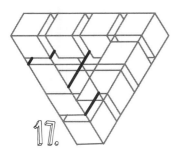

17.

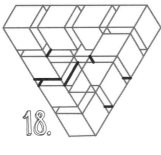

18.

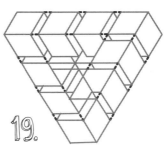

19.

Erase on
dotted lines.

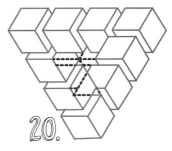

20.

Erase on
dotted lines.

21.

The line
drawing is
complete.

22.

23.

24.

Color in these cubes with different shades of gray.

TURNING THE PAGE

Make it look like a cartoon guy is turning the page. This one is pretty easy to learn how to draw. This is another one that will be fun to doodle.

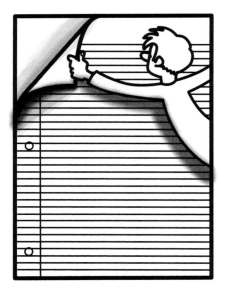

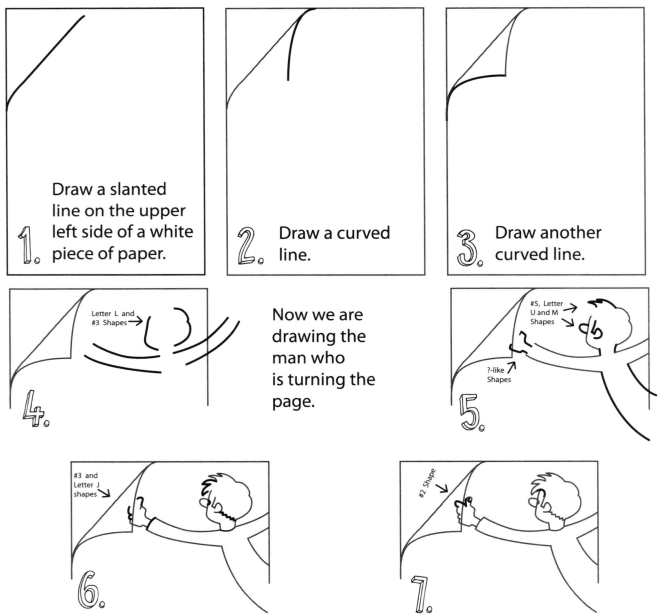

1. Draw a slanted line on the upper left side of a white piece of paper.

2. Draw a curved line.

3. Draw another curved line.

4. Letter L and #3 Shapes →

Now we are drawing the man who is turning the page.

5. #5, Letter U and M Shapes →
?-like Shapes ↗

6. #3 and Letter J shapes →

7. #2 Shape ↘

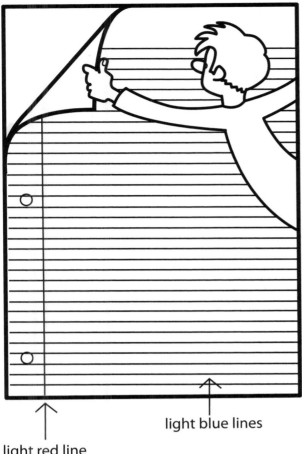

light red line

light blue lines

 Now draw the notebook paper's lines and holes. The lines that go across (horizontal lines) are light blue. The line going up / down (vertical line) is light red.

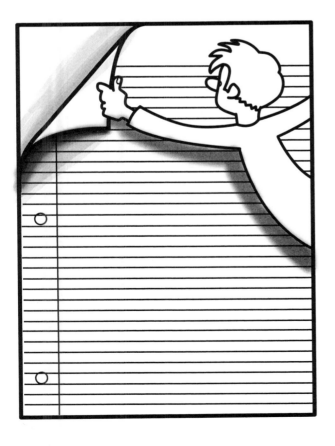

9. Now add shading on the left side of the man. Also add shading to the page curl. There is a shading lesson at the back of the book.

HOLE IN GROUND

Learn how to draw an incredibly cool hole in the ground. You can then put your homework and chores in there.

1. Draw random zigzags to form a shape sort of like this.

2. Draw some lines.

3. Draw some random lines for cracks.

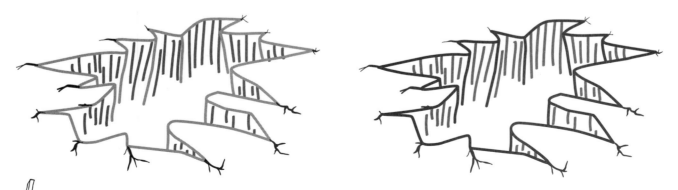

4. And draw some more lines of varying shades of gray.

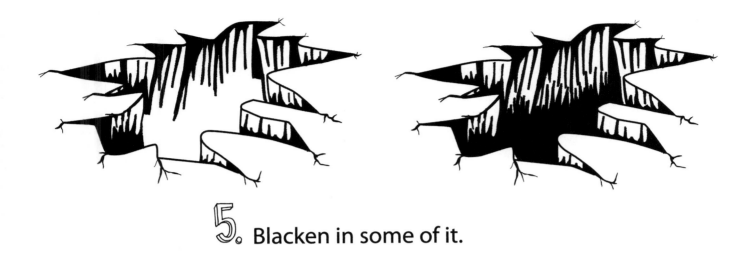

5. Blacken in some of it.

6. Shade in parts of it to make it look more realistic.

BOX LETTERS

Lightly draw your letters ... draw them any way you like. You might
want to draw them on graph paper...but this isn't necessary!

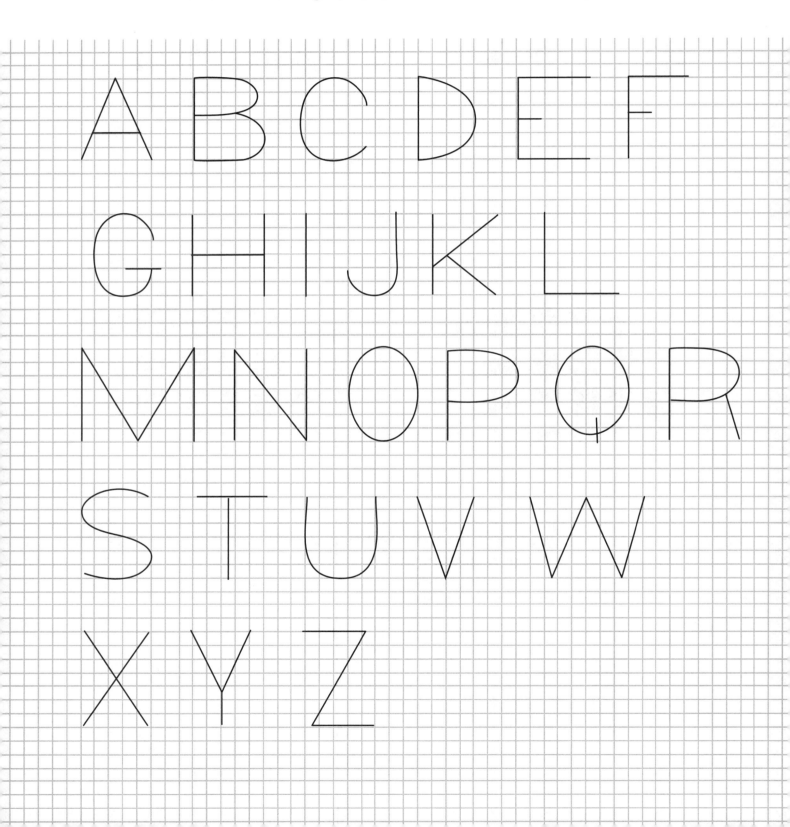

A B C D E F

G H I J K L

M N O P Q R

S T U V W

X Y Z

BOX LETTERS

This will be easy-ish for you if you are using graph paper. Outline the letters that you drew in the last step...use a ruler.

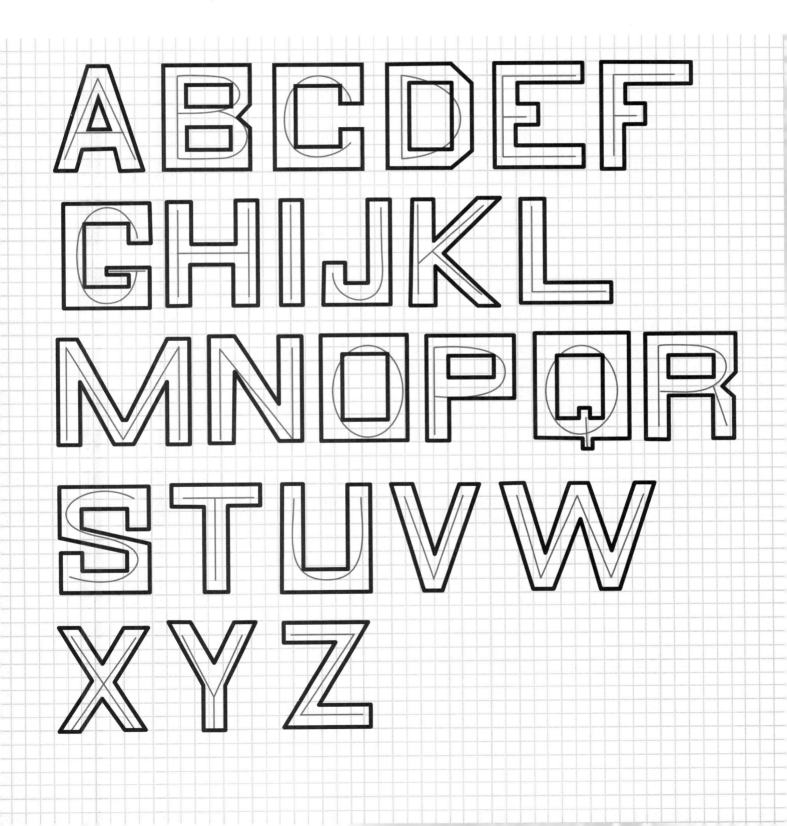

SHADING GUIDE

Here are some pencil shading tips.

Draw light lines, as you see to the left.

Add another set of lines, starting a bit to the right. You now made a slightly darker shade of gray.

Add another set of lines, starting a bit to the right again. Now there are 3 different shades of gray.

Continue doing this...each time starting further to the right.

OUR OTHER BOOKS

Please Give Us Good Reviews on Amazon! This book is self-published so we need to get the word out! **If You Give us a 5 Star Review**, and Email us About it, We Will Do a Tutorial Per Your Child's Request and Post it On DrawingHowToDraw.com